WHY YOU SHOULD NEVER SAY YOU ARE FINISHED

APOSTLE WISDOM U. J. N

Copyright ©: Wisdom U.J.N.
Publisher: Wisdom U.J.N.

ISBN: 978-0-7961-0571-4
First published: 2023
Print on demand.

TABLE OF CONTENTS

◆

DEDICATION

◆

This book is dedicated to Almighty God who revealed it to me and inspired me to write it. It is also dedicated to my beloved parents, the late Elder & Deaconess J. C. Nwokocha, channels through which God brought me to this earth.

I also dedicate it to my beloved wife, Prophetess Victoire, my biological children, my spiritual sons and daughters in our church and all believers in the world.

PREFACE

◆

There are moments in our lives we get to a crossroads or get stuck between the devil and the deep blue sea. Such moments could be during challenges in our quest for school admission, when we lost our job, are sick, when our marriage is not living up to expectation, or when we are disappointed in our relationship etc.

At such moments, we would naturally want to say we are finished. This is because when we look at our resources, our family background, our group of friends, we conclude that they will not be able to help us. If that is the point at which you are right now, *then,* rejoice because you are not finished. The truth is that, as Yogi Bara Ome stated, "It is not over until it is over!" It is not over for any living soul except you decide to throw in the towel. But so long as you keep struggling, it will only be a matter of time before you get to your destination.

Focus and persistency are key. In order to achieve his target, a good wrestler applies focus while wrestling with an opponent. A golfer does the same. When a driver loses focus while driving on the highway, it can cause a mishap. You stand as the driver for your success. Remain focused and avoid distractions to have unimaginable success. Challenges eventually fade away. The main reason one goes through challenges is to energize them to achieve success. Be focused and persistent.

This book is written to help you overcome your life's challenges and spur you on to achieve unimaginable success. It is written through the power, wisdom and inspiration of God Almighty who desires that all His children be successful. May God be praised in Jesus name! Amen!

ACKNOWLEDGEMENT

♦

All glory and honor be to God Almighty, my teacher, instructor, protector and inspiration who made it possible for this book to conceived, written and published.

I appreciate all men and women out there who have made a great impact on my life with the gifts of God. May Almighty God bless you all in Jesus name!

I will never forget the men of God under whose ministrations I have sat: Rev. Philip, Rev. Boniface Ubah, Pastor Chris Oyakhilome, my bishop, Bishop Matthew Egowa and many others. May the anointing of God in your lives never dry up!

My gratitude also goes to these people that gave out their time and attention for the success of this book:

Deacon Benedict Egbuliese, you encouraged me when I started writing this book and that gave me much courage to fire on; Mr. Boniface (Mr. Agitator), I am grateful for giving me your attention and time; Rev. & Rev. (Mrs.) Ubah (dad and mum, I am really grateful; may the good Lord reward you).

Last but not the least, my sincere appreciation goes to my beloved parents, channels through which God brought me to this earth; late Elder & Deaconess (Mrs.) Joseph C. Nwokocha. Dad and Mum, may your souls remain in the blossom of the Lord till eternity.

———✦———

CHAPTER ONE

CHALLENGES: THE GATEWAY TO SUCCESS

|

F irstly, I cannot write on this topic without giving you a definite definition of the word 'challenge'. It is a demanding task or situation. It can as well be seen as a new or difficult task that tests one's ability or skill. When one encounters more than one challenge, they become challenges. That is to say challenges are a sum of the obstacles in one's path. It is the plural of challenge. After having gone through the definition of 'challenge', I believe that this happens in life for the purpose of building up one's skill or future. Show me a successful person and I will draw your attention to the challenges they have gone through.

Life is full of challenges, struggles and experiences. Many have lost their hope in God due to the challenges they encounter in life. I was in a discussion with a man one day. He told me of the challenges he was facing in his family and said that he would be going to a juju priest to make findings. Happily, I used words of wisdom to discourage him from the mission he had set his mind upon. I am sure Almighty God knows everything he was going through and is able to deliver him. Remain faithful to God and never allow challenges blow you out of God's presence. God is able, and he will surely perfect his will in your life.

Challenges have made some people to believe that success is by luck, and not by God's grace. 1 Samuel 2: 7-8 says: "The Lord maketh poor, and maketh rich; he bringeth low and lifteth up; he raiseth up the poor out of the dust, and lifteth up the beggar from the dunghill, to set them among princes, and to make them inherit the throne of glory; for the pillars of the earth are the Lord's, and he hath set the world upon them'. Beloved, you cannot fail because God makes rich, and Jesus suffered that you may succeed.

Challenges are like an uncompleted house. It is a tedious experience at the early stage of building a house; the structure looks ugly and cannot be seen as a beautiful house. But once it is completed, it becomes a beautiful home to live in. A successful future may not be realistic if one runs away from challenges. For success to be achieved, there must be the existence of hurdles to be scaled. When one has this revelation, this insight, it enhances or even changes your mental disposition which helps you get to your destination.

I remember some years back when I finished my secondary school. I realized that there were needs in my home. My parents had seven children, and I saw that it would be cumbersome for my parents to see all of us through higher institutions of learning. I became restless like Esau in the Bible, when his father gave his birthright to Jacob, his younger one. He departed from his father to fight for his future and, as God would have it, he succeeded. I moved away from my parents to fight for a better future because I embraced this philosophy that I was not finished until God Almighty said so. Through the grace of God, I attended a higher institution of learning. That is what taking a decision can do. I never knew that my beloved mother, who was the major breadwinner of the home with support from our father, would be taken away so soon by the Lord who knows the beginning and the end. I would have felt it more when the breadwinner was no more if I had not left to fight for my future. Challenges in your background must not stop you; rather, think up and think *out* a solution; you have the power to create your world. Archbishop Margret Idahosa said, "You are born naked but you are not empty". Many great men in the world today were not born into plenty but they created plenty with their own hands. Don't quit so soon due to challenges but *quit* challenges to move forward.

One cannot desire to be successful in life without preparing for challenges. The road to destiny has never been smooth even when you have all it takes to get there. Challenges are all about running a race, and having to fight to see it through. Only the strong conquer! It is a race that offers one trophy to the winner. Challenges are the sacrifices you must make in life for success – except one has made them for you, like our Lord Jesus who redeemed us with his blood, set us free from bondage and gave us a victorious life.

In today's world, we have people enjoying their parent's investments because their parents had made sacrifices, they had paid the price. However, this does not mean that their offspring would not go through other challenges in life. The difference is the nature of challenges they might go through.

Joseph, a young Israelite, had a destiny to fulfill in the land of Egypt. The motivating fact in the story is that the young man refused to pay attention to the challenges present on the road to his destiny but was focused, positioning himself with his gift and power of vision. He did not take into account the problems he experienced. He humbled himself to learn, and God lifted him.

Most people today get tired early and quit when they encounter challenges. Don't quit because quitters never win. Challenges are like the school you must pass through in life. And, as a student, you must not be tired of learning. Never be afraid of challenges; rather rejoice and glorify God. It is He that will help you to graduate with a perfect record. Joseph graduated and became a man of authority in a foreign country. Let this be in your mind that greatness is ahead of you when challenges are around your neck. Challenges drive you to success; be focused and never sleep off on the journey. You are an 'original' and must not allow challenges to drive you into 'imitation'. The word 'imitation' can be an alternative and there is a possibility of it leading you to failure. Be a good photographer and have a positive image of your future.

Many went through challenges in the Scriptures and graduated with excellent records. I will mention but a few: people like Joseph, Daniel, Shadrack, Meshack and Abednego etc.

Sometimes, challenges make people get so worried that they begin to make bad utterances concerning their future. This has affected many lives, and caused them not to move forward or prosper in life. No one carries the cross without the crown. Behind every glory there is always a story. Never say you are 'finished' because God has not said so. Challenges should be seen as potholes and bumps on the road to success which can be crossed over by maximizing the potentials given to us by God Almighty.

God has not forsaken you when you are going through challenges. He has great plans for you; he desires good health and prosperity for all his children. You may ask "why then am I facing problems?" Many have taken wrong directions due to ignorance and disobedience to God's direction. The Scriptures say at Hosea 4:6 that, *"My people perish due to lack of knowledge"*. Sampson's problems led him to disaster because of disobedience (1 Kings 16). Others face challenges for the elevation of their faith in God who is preparing them for the next level.

Jesus encountered numerous challenges when he was on earth (Matthew 4:1-10). He was tempted by the devil. That means you too will also face temptations in order to live a victorious life. There are two kinds of challenges, spiritual and physical, which every follower of Christ must face on this earth. *"A man that is born of a woman is of few of days and full of trouble* (Job 14:1). The account of John (John 12:24-26) puts it thus: *"Verily; verily; I say unto you, except corn of wheat fell into the ground and die; it bringeth forth much fruit. He that loves his life shall lose it; and he that hates his life in this world shall keep it into life eternal. If any man will serve me, let him follow me, and where I am, there shall also my servant be. If any man serves me; he will get my father's honor.*

The search for quick blessings has driven many from one prayer house to another and they don't care to know the source of the power they are bowing to. The best prayer that attracts God is the one prayed faithfully, whether at home or in the church.

Some people spend their time and meagre resources on the internet looking for whom to defraud. You are jeopardizing your future, and also limiting your ability. Challenges must not lead you to such a life. Rather, set a good vision for yourself. Seek God's direction and move forward. The expectation of the righteous man will not be cut short but will manifest to the glory of God.

Gold becomes refined when it passes through fire, and it acquires the ability to stand the test of time. Don't allow today to swallow up the glory of tomorrow. When a trailer empties itself, it is a sign that it wants to take up a fresh load. If you have not stepped on any stone, you are standing alone. Heaven has made you a winner; don't give up before the time.

God spoke to Abraham in Genesis 17: 1 that: "I am the Almighty God, walk before me and be thou perfect, and I will make my covenant between me and thee, and will make and will multiply thee exceedingly". He did according to the voice of the Lord and became a blessing to many nations. You are the next to become a blessing to your generation if you can hearken unto the voice of the Lord. It does not take God time to lift you to your destiny. But seek first the kingdom of God and his righteousness and all other things shall be added unto you (Matthew 6: 33).

Having a negative imagination during challenges can give the devil room to achieve his goal in your life. He uses negative imagination as an active weapon to make people become failures. Always have a positive mental picture even in the midst of challenges, because your mental picture determines your physical outlook. Faithfulness to God Almighty, even when challenges seem unbearable, will surely give you resounding victory. In Daniel 3, we learn that the four young Hebrew men (Daniel, Shadrack, Meshack and Abednego) refused to bow down to the golden image made by King Nebuchadnezzar. They did not fear the burning furnace made to consume whoever disobeyed the king's command, and God gave them help which led to their victory. All hope is not gone when challenges are knocking at the door. Out of challenges comes greatness. God is not blind and neither is he deaf. He is aware of what you are going through. Take effective steps to conquer challenges, because the ability to conquer is what brings you victory.

How To Overcome Life's Challenges

A challenge had earlier been defined as a demanding task or situation. When one encounters more than one challenge in life, they are referred to as challenges. This can be seen as a race that has one trophy on offer for the winner. Challenges can be overcome if the following principles are observed:

a) Focus, Persist And Never Be Moved

b) Use the Re-Strategizing Technique

c) Look Beyond 'Happenings Within'

Focus, Persist And Never Be Move

This is an effective weapon with which to overcome life's challenges. Never lose focus because of a tedious or demanding task in the territory of your success. Continue to persist; the next move could be the last step to your victory. Persevere; discouragement must not be allowed a foothold in your life. It is one of the principles of failure. Life is a teacher; the longer you live, the more you learn. You are a student and you must not be tired of learning. A lecturer of mine normally says that when you stop learning, automatically you begin to decline. This is true. Science has shown that learning keeps your brain active and effective.

Challenges are like the wind that blows and stops after a moment. It blows off instability. You must be stable and focused as it blows in order not to be blown off from the point of your success. When you fail, try again. Don't stop because stopping means defeat. You failed in the past because you did not get the balance and more knowledge required to attain your goals.

A good wrestler applies focus while wrestling with an opponent in order to achieve his target. A golfer also does the same. When a driver loses focus while driving on the highway, it may lead to a mishap. You are the driver of your life and you must drive yourself to the point of your success. Remain focused and avoid distractions in order to have unimaginable success. Challenges eventually fade away. The main objective of life's challenges is to energize you to achieve success. Be focused and persistent.

USE THE RE-STRATEGIZING TECHNIQUE

When a technique or method that is applied to achieve a dream is found to be ineffective, it is time for you to re-strategize. It is not and has never been a wrong idea to start afresh. Most times, the best method to achieve success comes when a person fails and proceeds to try again. This means you must think, make corrections and repackage your method in a better form to achieve success.

Many scientists and great men in the world that we celebrate today failed several times before they achieved success. People like Michael Faraday (Father of Electricity), Graham Bell (inventor of the telephone), Marie Curie (discoverer of radioactivity) and Thomas Edison, who built the electrical bulb; and many others.

Getting information and advice from good sources can be helpful.

LOOK BEYOND 'HAPPENINGS WITHIN'

'Happenings Within' involves a situation one finds oneself in. These are the encounters in life which have the ability to jeopardize a future if negatively handled. It could be a distraction that pulls one out of the road to success. One could be unfocused due to this and may end up failing.

The 'Happenings Within' can be one putting much consideration in the present situation regardless of the future. Most times, this leads someone to being dependent in life. For instance, where a person born into a wealthy home ignores his dream due to satisfaction with his present circumstances. There is always emptiness when the available is used up. This is why it is not good advice to ignore a dream. You are a different person with a distinct gift, and you are created to be greater than your present circumstances.

Future generations and even people around us now will be negatively affected when we ignore our dreams. Dreams stand as empowerment to the future generation and others around us if actualized. The house of Jacob in the Scriptures would have died of famine if Joseph did not step out to achieve his dream.

Based on my statistical research, many families are going through difficulties because of the wrong foundation laid by the past generation. And no one has stood up to correct it. This chain will continue until one takes a step to break it. You are the best architect that can redesign the wrong structure designed by the past generation. No one has all that it takes – except you.

The future is infirm when there is much emphasis on 'Happenings Within'. It results in what I refer to as 'Mental Laziness'. This means one being unable to activate the creative mind. When the creative mind is inactive in a person's life, failure becomes the answer to the future. Your mental pictures determine the future picture. The level of your thinking gives you your position in life. Where you will be tomorrow is the result of decisions taken today.

If you are not comfortable with your present situation, you can change it to a better one, and activating the creative mind is the key. You have the power to create your world. God has given you the power. You must not limit your capability; rather, it should be seen as a platform to design a better world. Focus more on the future and disregard the happenings around you. Think of what to do to have a brighter future. You can break the chain of failure by disregarding the happenings and being optimistic about the future; not just being optimistic but also working hard to achieve your dream. You will surely achieve success.

CHAPTER TWO

THE CREATIVE ABILITY

The word 'creative' involves the use of skill and imagination to produce, work or manufacture something. 'Ability' simply means being capable of doing something. When the words are brought together, we get 'creative ability', which means the capability to use skill and imagination to produce, work or manufacture something.

After some research, I discovered that life cannot do without creative ability because it is crucial to success in life. God, being aware of this, never did away with creative ability; rather, he embraces it as His lifestyle and nature. Genesis 1 says: "*In the beginning God created the heaven and the earth. and the earth was without form and void; and darkness was upon the face of the deep. And the spirit of God moved upon the face of the waters. And God said, let there be light; there was light*. Read down and you will discover that God is the originator of creative ability; that is his nature. God began his work with creative ability and made a success of it. If you consider the scenario in Genesis 1, you will agree with me that success cannot happen without creative ability; they work together to produce a meaningful life.

Let's read together in verse 26 of the same Genesis 1: And God said; Let us make man in our own image, after our likeness: and let them have dominion over the fish of the sea, and over the fowl of the air, and over the cattle, and all the earth, and over every creeping thing that creepeth upon the earth.

Wow! What a wonderful creature the Lord made! You were created in the image of God; that's great! Do you know what that means? You have God in you! This agrees completely with Psalms 82: 6 which declares: . . . *Ye are gods!* . . . If that is the case, the creative ability, which is the nature of God, is also dwelling in you. If God created success out of it, you too can and should. The Scriptures make it clear that your success depends on the creative ability in you. No wonder the Bible says at Proverbs 18: 16 that the gift of a man makes a way for him.

Many fail today because they disregard their creative ability. They are living with what I call 'mental laziness', which means the inability to activate the creative mind. A creative mind or ability is critical to your success; that's why you must think positive in order to create positive things. What you think is what you create. The Bible says at Matthew 12: 34 that: *Out of the abundant of the heart the mouth speaketh*. Think right to create right!

According to the book of Genesis where we are reading, there are things that drive creative ability. They are:

a) Problems

b) Imagination

c) Action

PROBLEMS

According to Genesis 1, verses 2 and 3: *The earth was without form; and void, and darkness was upon the face of the deep; and spirit of God moved upon the face of the waters. And God said, let there be light and there was light.*

God saw this as a problem, the earth being empty and filled with darkness, and this triggered his creative nature to separate darkness from light and also to create other creatures to fill the emptiness of the earth. What problems do you see? The problem you see is the problem you solve. Regrettably, due to mental laziness, many emphasize solving irrelevant things that cannot lead or contribute to their success in the future. Some don't take the right steps, and they continue to pursue shadows in life.

God took the right step to achieve his plan. He did not start with the creation of creatures but first separated darkness from light which he spoke into existence. This is the first step and also the most important one to take before the others. Without light other creatures could not live comfortably on earth. A positive mental picture is what you need to influence you to solve relevant problems that can make you successful in life.

IMAGINATION

This means the ability to create pictures in your mind. It can be seen as the psychological way of dealing with an issue before taking physical action. God dealt with the emptiness and the darkness on the surface of the earth through his imagination before the actual activation of his creative ability. Light and creatures are the result of God's imagination. Imagination determines the action to take. You cannot move faster than your imagination; rather, your imagination spurs you to take action. Where one can reach in his or her imagination determines the course of his or her life. What you conceive in your mind is what you 'deliver' or become.

ACTION

Action is the physical step taken to deal with an issue. It is the final journey between a problem and your imagination. God said: *Let there be light and there was light*. It is not enough to imagine things but action should be taken to have a result. Vision minus action is equal to an illusion. In Genesis 1, God used two ways to achieve his creative ability.

a) Spoken word

b) Manpower

SPOKEN WORD

God called forth the light and other creatures to exist except man whom he took time to create. You can create your world by commanding that unfavorable situation to give way to your marriage, breakthroughs and other good things that you desire in life.

MANPOWER

In Genesis 1: 26 and 27, *God said: Let us make man in our own image, after our likeness; and let them have dominion over the fish of the sea and over fowl of the air, and over every creeping thing that creepeth upon the earth. So God created man in his own image; in the image of God created he him; male and female created he them.*

From the above passage, it is clear that God worked to create man. Man being created in the image of God has God's nature while other creatures were the result of the spoken word. You are God in human existence.

You must work to achieve that dream just like God did while creating man.

Laziness must not be allowed to rule your life because that amounts to failure! Don't be a dreamer only but also an achiever. One thing is to dream and another thing is to actualize it. When there is no force to achieve a dream, it becomes an illusion.

CHAPTER THREE

FEAR

|

The word 'fear' can be defined as fake mental pictures. It can also be seen as false events appearing as real. Fear is fake pictures and imaginations the devil uses to intimidate people. One living in fear can be defeated easily or destroyed by the devil. Fear makes a man to believe that witchcraft is after him when he sees an ordinary rat around his bed or even a butterfly. It also makes a woman, who woke up in the morning and saw marks on her body, begin to search from post to post for who was responsible for bewitching her.

Some allow the spirit of fear to conquer them especially when they have had terrible dreams. A person's fear energizes the devil to achieve his goal. Be a vibrant Christian and not a fearful one. It always makes people to lose their destiny of becoming successful in life; hence, they avoid taking risks.

Beloved, risk-taking is attached to success. If you desire to be successful, be a risk-taker. Every good thing has been made available for us right from the day we were created by God; but the spirit of fear makes you not to take your position. You have the ability to create success and just about every good thing you desire in life. Maximize your potential. Remember: *the gift of a man makes a way for him.*

"You are born naked but you are not empty". All human beings have special gifts deposited in them by God but some people have dumped theirs because of challenges or, probably, they do not believe something good can come out of those gifts. You are God's duplicate and if he is successful, you too must be successful. God said in Genesis.1: 26-28: *Let us create man in our own image, after our likeness and let them have dominion over the fish of the sea, and over the birds of the air, and over the cattle and over all the earth and over every creeping thing that creepeth upon the earth. So God created man in his own image, in the image of God created he them; male and female he created them. And God blessed them and said unto them be fruitful, multiply and replenish the earth and subdue it and have dominion over the fish of the sea and over the birds of the air and over every living thing that move on the earth.*

There are some important words used in the above verses and they are: Image, Dominion, Be fruitful and multiply. Being an Image of God means you are God's duplicate. God is creative; you must be creative as well. A child must be like their parents in one way or the other, either in character or in physical looks. You have God in you; stand up and possess your possession.

DOMINION

'Dominion', according to the Oxford Advanced Learners' Dictionary, is the authority to rule; control. Child of God, you have the authority to rule. Possess your possession and not live like a coward. Cowards always live in fear; such people have no direction or destination. Men of dominion always position themselves as kings. That's why Joseph refused to be deceived by the devil when he used Potiphar's wife to tempt him. He saw himself as a king, not a houseboy. Beloved, don't sit and make worrying or complaints your hobby. Stand up and possess your possession.

The devil does not want you to know your rights. The Bible says in John 10:10: The thief cometh not, but to steal and kill and to destroy, I come that you may have life, and that you might have it abundantly. The devil has come to destroy your position. Do not allow him because you will be empty if he actualizes his plans. As a real child of God, you don't have to fear the devil. According to Luke 10: 18-19: And he said unto them, I beheld Satan as lightning fell from heaven. Behold, I give unto you power to tread on serpents and scorpions, and over all the power of the enemy; and nothing shall by any means hurt you.

We have failed in using this power because of sin. A sinner always lives in fear and cannot confront the devil. Sampson lost his power because of sin and that opened the door for the devil to operate in his life. Dominion belongs to the righteous ones because they are superior to Satan; the lord Jesus has given them complete authority over the devil and his cohorts. James 4:7 says: *Submit yourselves therefore to God. Resist the devil and he will flee from you.* Therefore, beloved, reign in that greater revelation of your authority over him every day.

A person of dominion does not talk much or anyhow but chooses their words with care, because their speech is very valuable and has lots of wisdom in it. People like to pay attention whenever they speak because of the assurance of taking away good things out of their words. Such a person also does not mingle with everybody but chooses friends or companions wisely. Avoid friends that cannot positively affect your life. Do not live your life with confusion; rather, live as a person with authority.

Many believers always fear when they are seriously sick. This is ignorance! Speak the word; you have the power of healing. Some kill the power because of doubts. The Scriptures say in Mark 11:24 that *when you pray, believe that the Lord has answered*. As one who is born again, not only has Jesus given you power and authority to cast Satan out, he also made you superior to him and all his demons. The resurrection of Jesus gave you victory over him. This is confirmed in

Ephesians 2:6: *And hath raised us up together, and made us sit together in heavenly places in Christ Jesus.*

Beloved, you are seated with Christ, which means you are above principalities and powers, you are in control. It is now your responsibility to resist the devil and put him to flight. It is also your responsibility to frustrate his maneuvers and manipulations in and around you. When the devil holds you captive, as a Christian, command him with the name of Jesus and he will flee from you. You have the authority because you are a child of dominion. Dominating is what you are born to do, and everything around you is waiting to be dominated by you. What is happening around you does not matter; it is what is in you that does.

BE FRUITFUL, MULTIPLY AND REPLENISH THE EARTH

Have it in mind that there is no small gift. No matter how you may see it, every gift has great purpose to accomplish. God created it and put it in you and it is your responsibility to maximize it. You have the ability to multiply God's potential in you. Nothing can give you satisfaction apart from living according to the purpose of your being. God so much dislikes unfruitfulness; productivity is his nature. You can see this when Jesus said in John 15:1-2: *I am the real vine and my father is the gardener. He breaks off every branch in me that does not bear fruit and prunes every branch that does bear fruits so that it will be clean and bear more fruit.* You become a failure when you ignore the purpose why you live. Yet again, the Word of God says: *The gift of man makes a way for him.* Fear might have been a force in your life; but do not let the devil succeed in your life through fear. You would be truly 'finished' if you let him succeed.

CHAPTER FOUR

DISOBEDIENCE TO GOD'S WORD

The word 'disobedience' may be defined as one exhibiting disregard to an instruction or command given by a superior. Disobedience to God's word can now be defined as one walking contrary to or disregarding the word of God. This is an instrument the devil uses to get a believer. When he sows the seed of disobedience in your life, beloved, you are 'finished'. You will only be delivered by God's mercy. Success will be very far from you when you are in this kind of sin.

Maybe that is the genesis of the problem you are facing right now. Why not ask for forgiveness and turn back to God, so that the enemy will be put to shame? Note that whenever you ask God for something while in a state of disobedience, the devil will be busy reminding him that you are a disobedient child and that can make God not to grant your request.

Disobedience to God's word can as well cause marital delay, financial stagnation etc. In the gospel of John 21, some of the disciples of Christ abandoned the work Jesus left for them to do and went into fishing, following his crucifixion. They worked all night and caught nothing. Jesus, on encountering them in the morning, asked them to cast their net at the right side of the sea which they did, and caught a multitude of fishes.

Many fail today because they are spiritually blind, casting the net of their success at the wrong side of the sea as they refuse to obey the word of the Lord. The number one key to success is obedience to the word of God Almighty.

When Jonah disobeyed God, fish messed him up by swallowing him regardless of who he was. How very funny for a servant of God to be swallowed by fish as a result of disobedience to God's word! Disobedience to God's word makes you to lose your position and reputation with people and with God. You can be the General Overseer of a church, an Archbishop, Apostle, Prophet, great Evangelist etc. Once you disobey God's word, you will automatically lose your position until you reconcile with God.

Disobedience to God's word makes you to be faithless which is another tool the devil uses to capture believers. The devil uses doubt to make you not to be faithful to God's word in order to destroy your future or plans in life. When there is doubt or unfaithfulness in the life of a person, he cannot believe the words of prophecy and the promises of God in his word.

According to Hebrew 11: 1, *faith is the substance of things hoped for, the evidence of things not seen.*

The devil using his deceptive powers is ever busy trying to hinder people from having faith in God so that the desire of God in their lives will not be realized. He brings a lot of challenges to stop people from being faithful to God. He has strategies to achieve his desires. Beloved, do not give up because, if you do, you are 'finished'. Press on for God has great plans for you.

At a certain point in the travails of Job, his loved ones asked him to curse God and die, seeing his physical condition. But he ignored them and remained faithful to God. And God eventually doubled his blessings.

In the time of nothing, embrace giving as a responsibility. Giving is one of the key weapons we can use to defeat the devil. In 1 king 17:8-16, a woman of Zarephath who was a widow eliminated poverty in her family through giving. Some people do not believe that they can eliminate poverty through giving.

In Ecclesiastes 11, verses 1 and 6, we are instructed to: cast thy bread upon the waters; for thou shall find it after many days. In the morning sow thy seed, and in the evening withhold not your hand; for thou know not whether shall prosper, either this or that, or whether they both shall be alike.

It is obvious that, due to financial inability, some people have restricted themselves from giving. The word of God said that you should give and it shall be given unto you (Luke 6: 38). Don't give only when you are in abundance but try to share the little you have with others like the widow of Zarephath did. Never quit from giving because quitters never win or have any testimony in life. Refuse to be a failure because you are a victor! Be a faithful servant. Do not let today's seeming failure drive you to disobey God's word. Failure today can be a stepping stone to your greatness tomorrow.

In 2 kings 4:1-7, God proved his wonders to the wife of the son of a prophet, using his servant Elisha as a channel because of her faith. She ran to the man of God for a solution because she believed that God had the final say on her predicament. In the Scriptures, God remembered so many people and intervened powerfully in their lives because of their faith.

In the book of Esther, the Lord caused sleep to go out of the king's eyes because he wanted him to remember his obedient servant, Mordecai. The book of record was opened and therein was found the good deed of Mordecai – which he had not rewarded. Through that God destroyed the plans of Haman against the Jews. That is the reward for a faithful and obedient servant. I prophesy to you this day that the Lord will open a book of remembrance for you and the plans of the enemy (the devil) against you will be destroyed.

Do not be like the hypocrites that serve God because of the good things they have gained and still stand to gain from God. When there is a little challenge in their lives, they deviate from God. The devil thought that Job was that type, that is why he decided to try his faith in God.

Some people make huge donations to the church and give open service to God but they are not faithful servants. In times of challenges are when you know the true servants of God. Beloved, be of good cheer, remain faithful and obedient to God's word to have unimaginable success in life. Never allow persecution to drive you away from God.

CHAPTER FIVE

DISBELIEVING THE PROMISES OF GOD

|

'Disbelief' may be viewed as either the inability or the refusal to accept that something is true or real. In your walk with God, disbelief is very jeopardous and can kill. 2 kings 7:1-2 says: *Then Elisha said, hear ye the word of the Lord; thus saith the Lord, tomorrow about this time shall a measure of time flour be sold for a shekel, and two measures of barley for a shekel in the gate of Samaria. Then, a lord on whose hand the king leaned answered the man of God and said, behold, if the Lord would make windows in heaven, might this thing be? And he said, behold, thou shall see it with thine eyes, but shall not eat thereof.* That's what disbelieving the word of God can cause.

Don't ever doubt or disbelieve the word of God Almighty irrespective of whom the Lord is using to pass his message. Such unbelief is very dangerous and can attract the wrath of God. Be careful and never be deceived by the devil through his strategies.

In Genesis 17:16 the Lord said: I will bless her, and give thee a son also of her; you, I will bless her and she shall be a mother of nations; kings of people shall be of her. Then Abraham fell upon his face and laughed and said in his heart, shall a child be born unto him that is an hundred years old? And shall Sarah that is ninety years old bear? Although Abraham expressed doubt, the Lord did not take his doubt seriously because of the favour he had found in God's sight.

Beloved, it does not matter how long it might take; the promises of God must surely come to pass in your life! As the Bible says in Habakuk 2:3, *For the vision is yet to for an appointed time; but at the end it shall speak and not lie: though it tarry, wait for it because it will surely come; it will not tarry*. Again, Nahum 1:9 assures us: *What do ye imagine against the Lord? He will make an utter end: affliction shall not rise up the second time*. You serve a God of possibilities.

I remember a long time ago when I was arrested by the police in the city of Lagos, Nigeria, because of crossing the expressway instead of using the pedestrian bridge. The police pushed me into their vehicle with others that had violated the law, and took us to the station. Then I had no job and had very little money in my pocket. That day, I was coming back from the place I had gone to submit my Curriculum Vitae. When we got to the police station, the officers in charge asked each of us to pay some money for our bail. My fellow detainees haggled with the police on the amount demanded. I bent down my head thinking of what to do and how my people would feel when they heard that I was in police custody. I hadn't even up to five hundred naira on me, not to talk of giving them the amount they asked for.

When it got to my turn to pay the bail money, which was illegal to begin with, I told them that I hadn't any money except the little cash I had on me for my transport fare to my destination which was less than five hundred naira. Immediately, they became furious at me; one of them pushed me behind the counter. I began to shed tears praying to God to get me out of there; I didn't want my beloved family to be worried about me. About an hour later, one of the policemen came to the counter and collected the little money I had on me. He left me with the sum of one hundred naira and asked me to go.

Beloved, the Scriptures say in Matthew7:7-8: Ask, and it shall be given unto you; seek, and ye shall find; knock, it shall be opened unto you: for everyone that asketh receiveth; and he that seeketh findeth; and to him that knocketh it shall be opened.

Don't disbelieve the promises of God in times of challenges; rather, use them as references to enable you conquer. I decided to call on God because he said I should call upon him in the time of trouble; and he would deliver me (Psalms 50:15). God will never let you suffer in pain without showing up. Believe in him and you will surely have a testimony in Jesus name!

CHAPTER SIX

PRIDE

|

The word 'pride' refers to the pleasure or satisfaction that is gained from achievements, qualities or possessions. It carries two antithetical meanings that are both positive (virtuous pride) and negative (hubris pride). When it is wrongly applied, it becomes hubris which is arrogance. Being very proud or arrogant simply means one embracing the lifestyle and nature of the devil. He is very arrogant, proud and always desires that everybody on earth should live like him. He was thrown down from Heaven because of this arrogant attitude, and he has succeeded in imparting this attitude to many lives. In churches, you find the nature manifesting in the life of pastors and even of church members.

It is nice to show pride (of the virtuous kind) over a positive achievement; but it is quite unfortunate that some people exhibit it wrongly which amounts to hubris or arrogance; and this act has negatively affected many destinies. It makes one to lavish resources or waste their life. In the Scriptures, the prodigal son, out of hubris, asked his father to share his wealth and give him his own portion. His father did according to his request, and the young man went away and lavished all the wealth given to him within a short period. He ended up dining with the pigs instead of humans. One meant to be a prince descended so low to the extent of mingling with pigs in order to be fed. What a pity!

Depart from a friend that has hubris as it is very easy to contract. Nobody comes into your life and leaves you the same. Anyone that cannot add value to your life will definitely destroy the value in you. God does not pay attention to one living with hubris; rather, he pays attention to those with the spirit of humility. To have hubris is very dangerous; it can kill someone spiritually and even physically. It makes one to lie every time, and also leaves the person with no peace of mind. This can drive away people that God has positioned to lift you up. Stop this lifestyle because that is not the nature of God.

The devil tempted Jesus with hubris in Luke 4:5-7: And the devil said unto him, all this power will I give thee, and the glory of them: for that is delivered unto me, and to whomsoever I will I give it. If thou therefore will worship me, all shall thine. He claimed to be the owner of all those things but Jesus refused to bow down to him because he knew that the devil owned nothing. Arrogance is just his nature.

The Lord says in 2 Chronicles 7:14: If my people, which are called by my name, shall humble themselves and pray, and seek my face, and turn from their wicked ways; then I will hear from Heaven and I will forgive their sins, and I will heal their land. God is silent to many because of hubris. And they will continue to fail in life until they humble themselves, seek the face of God and turn from their wicked ways. Only then will God listen to their requests and do according to their desires. As the Bible has assured us in Proverbs 10:28, the expectations of the righteous result in joy but the hopes of the wicked will perish. Indeed, in Proverbs 23: 18, the Bible says that: For surely there is an end; and thine expectation will not be cut off. It will manifest to the glory of God.

The hubris species of pride has made some young men to live a deceptive life. They make unfulfilled promises to ladies to win their heart. Money does not grow in the hand of a proud person because he or she always spends it to gain respect from others. They don't accept advice from others. They believe they know it all. Beloved, that is the devil's nature. Please resist the devil and he will flee from you. An arrogant person loses good opportunities every time. He hates correction.

Jesus used a child to illustrate in the gospel of Matthew 18:1-4: At the same time came the disciples unto Jesus, saying, who is the greatest in the kingdom of heaven? And Jesus called a little child unto him and set him in the midst of them. and he said, verily I say unto you, except that ye be converted and become as little children, ye shall not enter into the kingdom of Heaven. Whosoever therefore shall humble himself as this little child, the same is greatest in the kingdom of Heaven. God is interested in the humble and dislikes ones with a proud nature.

The wise, which are the humble, always believe that their achievements were made possible by God; and these achievements are meant to affect lives positively. But the proud can be easily deceived by the devil that his achievements were attained by self-effort; and he looks at people that come around him for help as no-bodies. And he discards such persons if they did not show him acts of respect that border on worship. God said in the Scriptures that he will bring down the proud and raise the humble. Read Proverbs 10: 25 and James 4: 6.

Beloved; I pray that you possess the spirit of humility so that you will not be 'finished' in life in Jesus name!

CHAPTER SEVEN

THE POWER OF THE TONGUE

|

The tongue is found between the upper and lower teeth in a human being's mouth. Sometimes it acts as an active weapon the enemy uses to achieve his goal in a life; it depends on how you use it. Beloved, you are 'finished' if your tongue is negatively used. This is not a statement that is just being dramatic. The Bible informs us in Proverbs 18: 21 that: *Death and life are in the power of the tongue: and they that love it shall eat the fruit thereof.*

Some people make negative statements with their tongues and this has negatively affected their lives. Negative words have made many to live miserably. The tongue has a strong power over human life. Little wonder that even human laws have been made to control the use of the tongue. It can kill someone physically and spiritually if negatively used. It kills people's futures and destinies when used wrongly. Be mindful of how you talk or use your tongue because you can create failure or success through it. A word out of your mouth may seem of no account, but it can accomplish nearly anything or destroy everything! Remember that it only takes a spark to set an entire forest on fire.

Some people are suffering today due to the curses spoken over them by their parents. Reuben, the firstborn of Jacob in the Scriptures, suffered for many years due to a curse released on him by his father. God later used Moses to reconnect him to his destiny. I prophesy that

God shall reconnect you to your destiny through this book you are reading now in Jesus name!

Please, parents, stop speaking curses against your children. Rather, pray that God change their wrong attitude. The children's future will be affected by the words you speak over them. Negative words can result to a miserable life. Remember that children are the future. Negative words are a weapon in the arsenal of the enemy. John 10:10 says that: *For the devil cometh to steal, kill and to destroy*. He can achieve these through negative words.

Sickness has become some people's lot due to the power of the tongue. If you visit some people when they are sick and ask them how they are doing, their response would be: "My dear, I have spent a lot on this my sickness". Who told you that you own sickness? The Bible says we are healed by his stripes (Isaiaha 53: 5). Prophesy good health over your life and stop admitting sickness into your life. Sickness is not meant for you! The tongue is made for positive declaration and not for negative statements. Beloved, whatsoever you say will surely come to pass because you were made in the image of God; and as there is creative ability in God's tongue, so also is it in you. You must speak positively to have a positive result!

Some speak negative words through the influence of the devil. Resist the devil with your tongue and he will flee from you (James 4: 7). Prophesy prosperity, good health, breakthrough etc. over your life every moment. You must avoid friends that speak evil or negative words. The Scriptures say in 1 Corinthians 1:33 that: *Be not deceived; evil communication corrupts good manner.* Depart from negative-speaking friends so that you will not be contaminated with the negative mentality that they always give voice to.

Speak like a man of authority and never speak like a coward that always fears and cannot speak boldly. God has done so much for us but it is our responsibility to keep ourselves in his blessings. In Deuteronomy 30:19, the Lord told the children of Israel that: *I have set before you life and death, blessings and curses*. You have the power to create your future through positive declarations. Negative words sound like fire and can destroy a happy home.

As a Christian, you do not have to listen or pay attention to negative words because they can influence you emotionally. The door of life and blessings can be opened for you through the positive declaration that comes out of your mouth. And the door of death and curses can as well open for you through the negative statements you make. 1 Peter 3:10-11 admonishes us that: *For he that will love life, and see good days let him refrain his tongue from evil, and his lips that they speak no guile.*

Beloved, let us speak right with our mouth. Make a positive prophecy over your nation. Some people say that Nigeria cannot be a great nation. That is a negative prophecy. We need positive prophecies and faith to change the minds of our leaders to lead and govern us aright.

The tongue may be small, but it controls everything in your life. With it you can chart your course to a victorious life. God has given us the key to the windows of Heaven and it means we can use our mouths to unlock doors of blessings. He promises in Matthew 16:19 that: *And I will give unto thee the keys of the kingdom of Heaven, and whatsoever you shall loose on earth shall be loosed in heaven.*

Always let the words of God fill your mind because what is in your mind is what you speak! Matthew 12:34 says: *For out of the abundance of the heart the mouth speaketh.* And in the book of Proverbs 15:4, the Bible declares that: *A wholesome tongue is a tree of life.* There is no situation you cannot solve; speak the word of God over whatever you are going through now, and believe that the solution will automatically manifest.

PROPHETIC DECLARATION

Prophesy against Poverty, Sickness, Barrenness, Misfortune and Disappointment and whatsoever that troubles you with the word of God:

a) I am healed in the name of Jesus! It is written, by his stripes I am healed.

b) I am successful in Jesus name! God's word says that I shall be successful in whatsoever I lay my hand upon.

c) I am moving forward and shall never move backward in Jesus name!

d) I shall receive favour wherever I step my feet in Jesus name!

e) I shall never fall victim to any mishap in Jesus name!

f) Abundant life is my portion in Jesus name!

g) I can never fail in life but shall be successful in all my endeavors in Jesus name!

h) In my academics I am excellent!

i) Maritally I am excellent in Jesus name!

j) Etc.

All the above are your rights. Possess them and do not be afraid. Pray against negative words and order them to move out of your life. The tongue can make friends to become enemies. Physically and spiritually, the tongue is very vital in the human life. Use it right to have unimaginable success in Jesus name!

CHAPTER EIGHT

———✦———

SEXUAL IMMORALITY

|

The word 'sexual' involves male and female having sexual intercourse. It can also mean physical attraction or contact. It involves the fusion of male and female cells; while 'immorality' means not following accepted standards or due process of morals. Bringing the words together, we have 'sexual immorality' which can now be defined as deviating from the accepted standards of morality on sexual intercourse.

The devil has succeeded in sowing the lifestyle of sexual immorality in many lives in today's world. In fact, it has gotten to a point where people see it as part of fun. Many people have become shameless and do not regard it as sin any more, even in the church.

Some pastors have refused to preach the truth and choose to preach messages that suit, soothe and massage the sensibility of members because of money; they are wary of discouraging attendance of church programmes by members, experiencing numerical decrease of church members and what it means for their pockets. This has energized the members to continue dabbling in sin. The devil has possessed their heart to the extent of making them to forget the implication of their wrong deeds. Pastor, you must surely render an account of your deeds to God; even you, church member.

Note that once you venture into the sin known as sexual immorality, you automatically open the door for the devil to tamper with the potentials that God has endowed you with. Your destiny and your rights as a Christian will be easily affected by the devil. In the Scriptures, Sampson lost the awesome power of God in his life due to this sin. Read the whole of Judges 16.

Reuben, the firstborn of Jacob, lost his destiny because of sexual immorality. The Bible records in Genesis 49:1-4: Jacob called for his sons and said, gather round and I will tell you what will happen to you in the future; come together and listen, sons of Jacob, listen to your father Israel. Reuben, my firstborn, you are my strength of all my sons. you are like of my manhood, the proudest and strongest of all my sons. you are like ragging flood, but you will not be the most important for you slept with my concubine and dishonored your father's bed. Reuben lost his position and also his father's blessing because of sexual immorality, and that affected him physically and spiritually. Beloved; you must be careful.

Sexual immorality can make you lose your destiny and position in life. A lady was pushed out of her marital home by her husband because of the abortions she had committed when she was single. According to her, she terminated twelve pregnancies during her singlehood days; and when she got married, she was unable to get pregnant. The couple decided to go to the hospital to seek a solution, and the husband was astounded when the doctor told him that his wife's womb had become weakened and that, having been tampered with through several abortions, it was impossible for her to become pregnant again. The man looked at his wife with shock, because he trusted and loved her so much. A once happy home became a house of quarrels and misunderstanding. Sexual immorality is capable of making your future to be miserable.

Abortion has become a common thing in the eyes of some ladies today as the devil has blindfolded them. You may 'enjoy' it now but have it in mind that you are jeopardizing your future. Some ladies walk half naked on the streets all in the name of fashion; their mindset has been corrupted by the devil. They deceive themselves with this perception, "God is looking at the heart, not what you put on your body". Do not deceive yourself because that is an immoral dressing; and that dressing can lure your opposite sex into sin. Don't tempt your opposite sex for that is sin before God (read Romans 14: 21). Be decent in your dressing!

I boarded a bus one day on my way back from work. A lady who entered the bus with me was wearing a pair of trousers and a very small top. As she bent down to enter the bus, her top rode up her body while her trousers rode down her waist, exhibiting her buttocks before the public; and people were shouting. That was very indecent! Gone are the days when it was very difficult to see a woman's panties before her buttocks. Now you see the buttocks before the panties, and some do not wear any panties at all. They are controlled by the spirit of sexual immorality. There is nothing that destroys the future life of young ones more than the sin of sexual immorality. Satan does not fear or respect your spirituality or ministry if you open the door of sexual immorality. It is better not to dabble into it than to do so and later pray for remedy. The principal mission of the enemy (Satan) is to pull down and destroy believers, and sexual immorality is one of the most potent tools he uses.

One day, a lady told me that it is not a good thing for a young lady to maintain her virginity until she gets married. When I asked her the reason for her position, she said that it was because it will affect her adversely during child delivery. There is a lot that is wrong with her belief. But it suffices to say that it is undoubtedly a fallacy! Sadly, some ladies are living a life of sexual immorality because of this falsehood. Wow! The devil really knows how to put lies into people's mind in order to deceive them. Beloved, do not be deceived: children are from God Almighty and he alone knows how to bring the child out of the womb in due time. Women put to bed through the grace of God, and not by their, might or the amount of sex they had or did not have before or after marriage.

Sexual intercourse is even committed in the street these days. Very shameful! What God has prepared for couples, the unmarried taste it before marriage and that has hindered many of them from getting married and even them deprived of good things! Many ladies turn to the church in order to get married after many years of swimming in the ocean of sexual immorality. They pretend to be committed Christians while their motives are anything but pure. However, you need to know that, while you can deceive men, you cannot deceive God! Repent and confess your sins to God Almighty and he will show you mercy and grant your desires.

When a man deflowers you as a lady, both of you have entered into a blood covenant. As a man puts his organ inside you, his organ will be wet with the blood that comes out of you following the rupture of your hymen. That is why you are not supposed to carelessly allow any man to take your virginity as a woman. If you have fallen a victim to this, ask for God's forgiveness and pray for deliverance from an evil covenant, and the evil spirit that you might have contracted through sexual immorality.

Many people are undergoing difficulties today because of sexual immorality. Most of them probably fornicated with men and women that are possessed with evil spirit while some have been initiated into evil kingdom through it as well. Beloved, you do not know the kind of spirit that dominates in the life of the person you fornicate with.

A man that always desires to have sex with you when both of you are not married to each other is not your real husband but an agent of destruction. Depart from such a person and seek God's direction. The intention of some men is to have sex with you and dump you; and if you start your life with such a man, you are finished. You will become a waste bin where men dump their refuse and walk away except God intervenes in your life. Ladies note this: not all men that say "I love you" really love you. Some just like your body and want to have sex with you and then dump you. Don't be carried away by fake expressions of love by men or the sweet words with which they talk to you. Most times, it is deceptive. Don't under-value or even disvalue yourself before them; rather relate with them with wisdom.

A lady who was in a relationship with a young man thought that her so-called fiancé was going to marry her. Unknown to her, the young man had a different agenda. As the relationship went on, she got pregnant and then informed her fiancé. Unfortunately for her, the young man rejected the pregnancy and asked her to abort the child. She did as the fiancé suggested, just to please him; and that ended the relationship. This is one of the wages of sexual immorality.

Those of you in ungodly relationships must be care-ful; seek God's direction so that you will not depart from his will. Having sexual intercourse before marriage is fornication, and the Scriptures say that fornication is a sin (1 Corinthians 6:9).

Women have been one of the challenges I face in life; but I thank God for his grace upon me. God has been helping me to conquer every time because of my covenant with him. Beloved, you need the grace of God to overcome the sin of sexual immorality because it is not easy to quit it. Pray for God's forgiveness and his grace to overcome it as well. Let the spirit of God control your mind. Rev. Dr. Olukoya said in one of his books that fornication is a sin as grave as adultery because it affects the future marriage and eternal fate of the victim. It is a destiny destroyer and the spirit of God does not work with a fornicator. Move away from it so that your future will be bright and shiny like a star.

People were punished with death in Old Testament times due to fornication. But, now, many people believe that God is no longer taking action because of grace. You must surely receive eternal punishment from God someday if you refuse to desist from and repent of it. Every sin that a man does is without the body, but he that committed fornication sins against his own body (1 Corinthians 6: 18). 2 Corinthians 3:16 says: *What? Know ye not that your body is the temple of the Holy Ghost which is in you? Which ye have of God, and ye are not your own? For ye are bought with a price: therefore, glorify God in your body, and in your spirit, which are God's.*

In the scriptures God seriously emphasizes the sanctity of your body and that really means your body is vital to God Almighty. It is the dwelling place of the Holy Spirit. It is thus very dangerous for one to defile it. It is expensively made by God for his own glory.

One night, years ago, I was passing through a motel and saw ladies standing at different corners of the building waiting for men. What an abomination! Some people do not respect the hand work of God anymore. 1 Thessalonians 4:3-4 says: *For this is the will of God, even your sanctification, that ye should abstain from fornication, that every one of you should know how to possess his vessel in sanctification and honour.*

The will of God is for you to shed this nature because is not his; rather, it is the nature of the devil. God's nature is holiness and that is why he demands the sanctification of your body. If you have gotten to the age of marriage, go into it and focus on your wife or husband; for marriage is approved by God. 1 Corinthians 7:2 states that: *But because of the temptation of sexual immorality, each man should have his own wife or each woman should have her own husband.*

Refuse to be deceived by worldly information; rather, listen to and follow the directions of God so that your future may be bright. You are made to be great and it will only manifest if you follow God's directions.

CHAPTER NINE

HAVING A VISION

The word 'vision' means the ability to see, or to think about the future with imagination or wisdom. Many have failed in life because they do not have the time to imagine or look into the future; rather, they prefer to depend on someone to be successful. This is dangerous!

If your relatives are wealthy, do not depend on them to succeed. Think about how to become successful like they are. You have the power if only you can obey the principles of success. Success is not made for a particular group of people; rather, it can be attained by anyone who truly desires it.

Positive thinking towards having a great future is crucial in life. It is among the principles of success. Do not think that success falls from heaven; it is one's responsibility to create it. Some people are wont to say, "Do not think about tomorrow, it will take care of itself". This is a deceptive comment some lazy people comfort themselves with. Let us not deceive ourselves: to have positive thinking about tomorrow is very necessary. According to Matthew 16:19, the power of the kingdom of Heaven has been given unto us. We have the power to create the future.

God made a remarkable statement in Genesis 1:28 when he said: *Be fruitful and multiply and replenish the earth*. God has done his own work by creating you and making available all the facilities you need to be successful. We have all it takes to be successful in life.

Reposition your mind to positive things and good plans.

You are like a photographer and need to have an image of your future. Have positive mental pictures; they determine your physical pictures. You cannot live above your thinking faculty! Think big and take effective action to actualize it in your mind. Success does not come until you walk and work towards it.

TWO FACTORS REQUIRED TO ACTUALIZE A VISION

a) Allowing God to direct your mind

b) Ability to follow your mind

It is very important to allow the God that created you to direct you. Do not be faster than your own Maker! Be ready to follow the directions God will give you to achieve that vision.

We celebrate some great people in the world today that never allowed their vision to die irrespective of their challenges; people like Graham Bell, who invented the telephone we use today, Michael Faraday, the father of electricity, and many others. It is very bad when one refuses to have a vision in life. As I had said before, your vision or dream is a good platform for the next generation.

People that God created to be great are now beggars, slaves and swimming in the ocean of poverty because they lack vision. Some even blame God for their misfortunes, not knowing that they are the cause. While others that had a vision killed it because they saw their family background as an excuse to not be successful. If you consider your family background a problem that is hindering you from actualizing your vision, you are 'finished'.

You must take risks for your vision to come through. Risk-taking is the number one principle of success. Elisha followed his master Elijah to his departure point. They passed through River Jordan by the application of the spiritual wisdom of his master. Elisha did not mind how he would cross the river on his way back but followed his master because he had a purpose to accomplish. God brought him back safely. Here was a man who was ready to take any step to succeed, no matter how tedious or perilous it might be.

Fulfillment is your destination, and you only get there by following God's direction. Believe in God and believe that everything is possible to those that trust in him. Letting your dream or vision die is a tragedy and is capable of bringing disgrace to your future. Nurture your dream, apply manure to it, so that it may grow as quickly as possible and make you successful.

Prayer for the future is excellent but, when you pray, you must take action in faith in order to have answers to your prayers. Beloved, an idle mind is the devil's workshop – just like an idle hand is a recipe for poverty and failure.

Hard work is another principle of success and it is capable of giving your background the shape you desire.

Work hard; it is God's will for you to prosper in whatsoever you lay your hands upon (Psalms 1: 3). Pray and move forward, you will experience God's miracle. Laziness is very bad and should never be encouraged. A lazy man or woman cannot be successful; and they always think that the successful ones made it by luck. Beloved, hear this: being a Christian is very good but don't have it in your mind that you can be successful if you avoid God's direction and do not take action to achieve his direction.

Hard work is so important and laziness so frowned upon that the Bible says at 2 Thessalonians 3: 10: that, *For he that does not work will not eat.* Hard work is very important to achieving a vision. When there is no force or action towards a vision it becomes an illusion.

In my view, success can be defined as the ability to think up or *out* what others need, and make it available to them while they give you what you want – which could translate to material gains. Maximize your potential for that is your success.

Another principle of success is to avoid friends that cannot contribute positively to your vision. Such people are called vision killers and can destroy your vision if you relate it to them. A friend that cannot make a positive contribution to your vision should be changed before he or she changes your vision.

FACTS ABOUT VISION

a) Positive thinking

b) Risk-taking

c) Disregarding your background

d) Positive thinking

The level of your mental thinking determines the level you will get to in life. Having a positive mindset about the future helps to change an otherwise average or even miserable background. Napoleon Hill wrote a book titled *Think and Grow Rich*. The thesis of the book is essentially that becoming rich or wealthy in life depends on the thoughts in one's mind. You cannot be greater than the contents of your mind because the mental pictures you generate have implications for the physical things that happen around you. Thinking positively about the future is thus a major factor in any vision.

You are the architect of your future because that future is based on the image you designed. The amount of exertion you put on your mental faculty determines the result you'd get. Again, you have the power to recreate your world through positive thinking because you have the creative license through God. You do not need to be frightened by anything, especially the future. Life cannot always give you what you want; it only gives you what you force it to surrender to you. If you are in an uncomfortable state, you can change it by thinking up the solution. The solution is in you; make use of God's ability in you.

There are many unemployed youths in the country today due to the fact that they fail to have a vision for their future; rather, they choose to be dependent. Others went to school with the mindset of having white-collar jobs after graduation. School is the best place to set a vision for a better future. Think of being a boss and stop thinking of remaining a servant.

Like I said, success only comes when you can satisfy people's needs with what you have; and their response to the value you create determines your satisfaction level. For instance, Michael Faraday discovered that humanity needed electricity to operate in life. He sat down and thought about how to invent electricity. Graham Bell saw the need for communication over a distance; he expressed the ability in him by inventing the telephone we are enjoying today. Do not limit your mental ability. You can change your world with it. When you fail to imaginatively create the future through the power or gift that your Creator deposited in you, you are mentally lazy, and God is not glorified in it.

RISK-TAKING

There is always fear of loss when having a vision; that is, the fear that potential failure can generate. But you must not give in to it. Take a step forward to actualize your vision. If you are frightened of taking risks to actualize a vision, you are simply afraid of becoming successful in life. Risk-taking gives rise to rapid success – just like it was for Elisha who followed his master to his departure point, not minding the challenges on the way. He ended up grabbing what he wanted: a double portion of what a mighty prophet like Elijah had. You need to take risks in order to actualize your potentials because you cannot have all you need to actualize it until you take a step forward. Nothing can give you joy, greatness and rest in your mind except you live out your purpose in life. As the Bible says and we have also seen in action throughout history, the gift of a man opens doors for him.

God has created everything you need to become successful. Don't limit your capability. You can change your world because you are the image of God and carry his divine ability. You possess creative powers emplaced in you by God Almighty. Take a step to actualize your potentials, and stop being afraid of the unknown. Risk-taking is the number one principle of success. God is with you and it is your responsibility to work hard to develop the gift of your Maker in you.

DISREGARDING YOUR BACKGROUND

A vision can never be actualized when one's family background is seen as a problem. You must not allow your family condition to influence your mental ability to generate a vision because it will place limitations on your ability. Take a step forward to make your vision well packaged. The ways to actualize it will surely come if you take a step forward without being in two minds.

Everyone in this world was created to be great. Sadly, many have allowed their vision to die because of fear. It could be fear of having no money to actualize the vision. Or the fear of being thrust into the eye of the public. Or some other reason. First of all, money is not and should not be the priority to achieving a vision. The priority is to package the vision properly. When a vision is well packaged there will be a way to achieve it. You must not allow your family conditions to stop your vision because you are 'finished' if you do so.

Everyone must not be born into wealthy homes. Some are born into average homes while some are born into places where money is a rare visitor. In such circumstances, it becomes your responsibility to recreate your world by maximizing your potentials. No one can change the conditions of your background except you. You were not created to remain like that. You must take a step forward, not backward.

SIX THINGS TO DO TOWARDS THE ACTUALIZATION OF A VISION

a) Define your vision

b) Believe your vision

c) Draw techniques to actualize your vision

d) Be focused

e) Make use of any opportunity you have

f) Avoid sentimentality when trying to actualize your vision

Define Your Vision

The ability to define, know and also have an adequate understanding of a vision helps you to find a way to actualize it, no matter the challenges in your path. When there is an inadequate understanding of a vision, the road to succeed with such a vision becomes difficult. Never choose a vision based on the success of others with regard to a similar vision. An adequate understanding of a vision is very paramount. Always create chance for yourself to think about your future, and listen attentively to the positive ideas your mind gives you.

Believe Your Vision

The size of a vision does not matter, what matters is its actualization. No matter how small a vision may seem to be, it can change your background if actualized. Sometimes a vision comes in a smaller form but expands in the process of its actualization. So, you must believe in your vision.

Draw Up Techniques to Actualize Your Vision

When a vision is adequately understood, and full confidence is expressed in it, the next thing to do is to draw up techniques to actualize the vision. For instance, you must know how much is involved and other things needed to actualize the vision. Strategize and set up goals on how to get the things required. Do not forget that the first step you must take is to properly package your vision. How you package your vision matters a lot, because a well packaged vision can attract helpers. Do not welcome mental laziness because of the ugly conditions you may be into. It can make your future to be miserable. Also, never allow your vision to die; you are finished if it does.

Be Focused

A driver always puts much concentration in his work while on the highway to avoid mishap. You are the driver of your vision. And a vision always goes to where it is driven to. You must be focused and not be distracted by anything. Continue the journey, and mind the challenges on the way. Let your eyes and mind remain focused. This is because being unfocused can destroy the vision or draw you back to step one.

Make Use of Any Opportunity You Have

You must make use of any opportunity you have to actualize your vision. Do not procrastinate, because you may not have the opportunity again. Time wasted might be destiny lost. You may only have one opportunity in life. That's why an opportunity must not be played with. Any opportunity you meet must be grabbed with both hands to avoid regrets tomorrow.

Avoid Sentimentality When Trying To Actualize Your Vision

In the process of vision actualization, sentimentality should be pushed to the very background. To please a relative and lose a vision is very unfortunate. If a relative's contribution to your vision is not favorable to its actualization, the contribution must be set aside.

Getting advice or support from relatives or friends is not bad, but you must be selective. Sentimentality can warrant the following:

a) Failure

b) Poverty

c) Disappointment

d) Death

THINGS THAT CAN END A VISION

a) Mental laziness

b) Mingling with the wrong people

c) Fear of risk-taking

d) Inadequate funds

Mental Laziness

Like I said about this term, mental laziness, it is a situation in which one is unable to activate the creative mind. How much you think determines how much action you can take in life. And the action determines the result you get. Many people continue swimming in the ocean of poverty because they fail to use the creative ability they are endowed with by God Almighty. Napoleon Hill wrote a book titled *Think and Grow rich*. The level of your thinking determines the level of your growth in all ramifications. God is a creator and you are made to be creative as well because you were created in his image and nature. Do not get tired of thinking positive things because they influence your action.

Mingling With The Wrong People

No one comes into your life and leaves you the same; either they add value to you or they diminish or even destroy the value you have. That is why you must be careful with the people you mingle with to avoid missing the track to your destiny.

Fear Of Risk-Taking

Fear was earlier defined as fake or false events appearing as real. Fear of risk-taking simply means one avoiding action to achieve his vision. Vision minus action is equal to an illusion. When you avoid taking a step to achieve your vision due to fear of loss, my dear, you are already a failure. Great things are not done by impulse but by the series of small things brought together. Great works are performed not by strength but by perseverance. Great work is done by people who were not afraid to become great. You cannot be great or achieve vision when you are afraid of taking risks.

Inadequate Funds

This simply means a situation where one does not have enough money to achieve their vision. This situation always weighs people down. But like I earlier said, money is not a priority in achieving a vision. The priority is giving the vision a good packaging which may attract helpers. Do not leave the vision empty; package it well and, in due time, you will surely achieve it. The Scriptures say in Habakuk 2:3: *For the vision is yet to for an appointed time; but at the end it shall speak and not lie: though it tarry, wait for it because it will surely come; it will not tarry.*

CHAPTER TEN

WORKING ON YOURSELF

|

For you to record timely success in life, what exactly should you be working on? Very many of us are not quite satisfied or happy with life. We do not like how we live. We do not like the quality of our lifestyle. We do not like what we earn or where we live. We are generally frustrated with our needs gap and insufficiency in life. We increase the intensity of our labour and number of manhours. Yet it appears that the more we work, the tougher things get. Many of us sacrifice our time of rest, our time to socialize, our time with our family, our time of service to God, even our time of sleep all for work. But with all this sacrifice, things do not appear to be getting any better. We look around and observe other people who seem not to be working as hard as we do but are living better. We become confused, discouraged and, at times, envious while wondering what is wrong with us.

The reward for hard work is success. What can we do? We wonder what the secrets of success and financial sufficiency are. Beloved, you cannot improve your circumstances in life without improving yourself. Perhaps, the reason you are struggling in life is simply because you are working very hard on something instead of working hard on yourself. To get impressive results on your labour may not be as a result of what you do or how hard you do it or where you do it. It is actually how well you do it. How well you do it, however, is a function of how good you are at it. Every profession in this world has produced billionaires and has the capacity to continue to produce billionaires. There are billionaire doctors, billionaire fashion designers, billionaire stylists, billionaire lawyers, billionaire shoemakers etc. Success in any endeavor is really not in the quantity of work you do or the number of hours you work. It is in the quality of your performance and excellence at what you do. To work less and earn more, you must be the best or one of the best in your profession. This makes it possible for you to charge and earn very much per project than most of your colleagues in the same business or profession.

Money is earned and not just made. Financial success in life is possible beyond just making money. You should learn how to earn money. You are yet to earn most of what you chase and are yet to obtain and also cannot retain. There is nothing wrong with desiring good things but it is not okay to be desperately desirous of something you are yet to earn.

What are those things you really want for your business, career or life? Have you earned them or you just want them? Do you deserve them? Probably, you want the following:

a) A good job

b) Good income

c) A good spouse

d) Good kids

e) Good friends

f) A good life

g) Happiness, etc.

Dear friend, there are some things you can't earn in life until you are qualified for them. And you can't qualify unless and until you pass your test in this area of life. You must qualify to earn all these good things you want in life. They cannot come to you simply by your wanting them. You must earn them legitimately for them to arrive and abide. Ladies and gentlemen, the most important area in life to put in the hard work is yourself. If you have been confused as to why all your hard work has not brought you the desired result, it is because you are perhaps working too hard on things and neglecting working on yourself. You cannot be rich and successful by chasing success and riches. You can only be rich and successful by attracting success and riches, that is, making them come to you. You must work very hard on yourself so that success and riches can locate you and remain with you.

Live life with character, regarding anything you want in life, before it can be released to you legitimately. When you fail life's tests in any area, you will not get that which you want in that area. Life will withhold it until you pass the tests. To get a good job, you must be a fantastic and outstanding candidate. To earn good income, you must be a very good employee. To become a leader, you must first be a good servant. To attract a good life partner, you must be a good life partner yourself. To raise good kids, you must be good at parenting. To enjoy love and respect, you must give love and show respect to others. Anything you want to get in life, you must first become.

If you know in your heart that you have not been doing all these, I am afraid you lack the credentials. Are you expecting things you have not even earned? Do not get me wrong: it is okay to work hard on things, but start working harder on yourself. When you grow in character and excellence, you will attract good success. Character and excellence of skills are key to enduring success and riches. You must work very hard daily on your character and your skill: sharpen one and grow in the other. Growing in character is the ability to choose what is right over how you feel every time. It is called discipline. The more you go for what is right instead of what you like, you develop in character. Following your feelings will fail you. Doing the right thing, even when you don't feel it, will enhance your value.

It is time to start reading great relevant materials online and offline. It is time to start listening to messages and teachings by top leaders that can transform your thinking, career, business and life. You need to stop listening to the type of music and other things that can corrupt your thinking. It is time you begin to attend meetings and follow people that will help you grow. Avoid those that cannot positively impact your life. Take responsibility for your character development. At the end of the day, you will render your account to your Maker and your excuses or apportioning of blames to some other persons won't help you. Dear friend, work on the right things. Work on yourself.

Tips To Succeed

   a) Listen more and talk less

   b) Be hardworking and not lazy

   c) Be humble

   d) Be honest

   e) Be truthful

   f) Be dependable

g) Seek support for difficult areas of life

h) Appreciate people

i) Treat people fairly and equally

j) Keep your greatest secrets to yourself

k) Be focused, determined and disciplined

l) Have the fear of God

m) Be responsible

n) Do not look down on people

o) Respect everybody equally

p) Read positive and spiritually uplifting books

q) Don't be afraid to take risks to achieve a vision

WORDS OF ADVICE

a) Your best friend can be used to set you up; so, be careful of the friends you tell your secrets or vision to;

b) Create a good reputation for yourself; don't give others a good reason to think badly of you;

c) Mind your speech while in public; your comments might build up or destroy your future.

God bless you as you do all these and more. You must succeed!

ABOUT THE BOOK

There are moments in our lives when we get to the crossroads or get stuck between the devil and the deep blue sea. Such moments could be during challenges in our quest for university admission, when we lost our job, are sick, our marriages are not living up to expectation, we are disappointed in our relationship etc. This book is the remedy for such situations and was written through the grace of God Almighty to help you overcome challenges and have unimaginable success.

ABOUT THE AUTHOR

The author is a native of Egbelu Okpurulor Umueze Autonomous Community, Chokoneze in Ezinihitte Mbaise Local Government Area of Imo State, Nigeria. He attended Kings College, Lagos, but obtained his Senior School Certificate (SSC) at the National Technical College, Oyigbo, Rivers State. He also attended the Lagos State Polytechnic where he studied Business Management. He is the third child but first son of his late parents.

In order to fulfill his divine calling, he obtained a ministerial ordination certificate-cum-license through *Alpha and Omega Ministerial Association* (an arm of *Alpha and Omega Theological Seminary*) and was ordained an Apostle. He is presently the Lead Pastor of *Champions in Christ Int'l Ministries*, and is the Co-

Founder and President of many non-denominational Christian associations including *Champions Word Outreach International* and *Heavenly Mandate*.

Apostle Wisdom is a preacher of the Gospel, a filmmaker, screenwriter and actor. He is married to the beautiful Prophetess Victoire Wisdom with whom he is blessed with children. They live in Johannesburg, South Africa.

To reach the author, please follow any of these links.

Email: wisdomjoseph513@gmail.com.

Phone Contacts: +27731630215, 0638337567

NOTE